My Baby Died. Where Is My Baby?

Clayton B. Carlson

Table of Contents

The death of a baby is one of the biggest sorrows for a parent. The heartache from the loss can linger and for some, they can never escape it. Different cultures and religions have varied explanations for where the deceased child may be. Doing a search of major world religions will yield a wide array of beliefs. Beliefs from the baby being safe with Jesus, or already in the fires of hell, to it getting ready to be reincarnated as its karma dictates. Other beliefs may put them into the cosmos as a star or a planetary body. There is no lack of choices out there waiting for your consideration.

A modern evolutionist, or atheist would most likely say the baby is dead and at best their energy will go on to other life forms, similar to any other creature that dies. For they believe people are at the top of the evolutionary chain and fundamentally no different than the animals they have progressed beyond. They feel a person's life has no future beyond death. The atheist's, or evolutionists answer to a grieving parent would be a short one, not holding out any future for the dead child.

Virtually all of mankind has historically had some belief or legend of an afterlife. The grieving parent may well get bewildered with all of the options to believe in. In the midst of an emotional storm is not the time to be building your boat of faith. Often though, we never put our faith to the test until we are in the midst of the tempest. At times it may seem like our ship of faith will be torn apart by life's storms. As a rule, it's not until we need to be sure of what we believe that we start to prove the answers given to us. That proving strengthens our faith hope and trust, which are vital elements in everyone's lives. They are basic to the human psyche regardless of your beliefs.

Faith for Christians is important. For it is through faith in Jesus we believe we gain salvation. Hope for humans is important. For it is hope that will keep us motivated throughout life. Trust for mankind is important for personal psychological wellbeing. We use it to know that our beliefs are well established on firm foundations. Without these elements in our lives we can start to feel like we have no solid anchor points on which to cling. Being strong in all three of these emotional building blocks, faith, hope and trust, is fundamental to our mental health. They can help us be joyous, contented people. For the religious along with the atheist, we will all use some of these three fundamental supports in our lives.

The atheist or evolutionist may be the first to bristle at the thought of having faith. They will point out that their beliefs lie in facts and science, not in faith. They may go on to say faith is blind, that you should not trust, what you are hoping in is correct, but that you need to have the verifiable facts to prove it. They would like others to be more like themselves, trusting only in the facts of science. Their faith in the scientific method shows them their hope is firm and well rooted in the trustworthy facts of science.

What exactly is the scientific method and how does it give them such trust? Here are some results from a quick online search for a definition of the scientific method.

Scientific Method

noun

Scientific method is a well documented, carefully controlled experiment that applies logic, order, and critical thinking skills to solving problems and finding new information.

Steps to the Scientific Method

1. Ask a question to define the problem or issue you wish to resolve.

2. Do background research to learn what others have discovered about your topic.

3. Construct a hypothesis to determine how you think your questions should be answered.

4. Test your hypothesis by conducting an experiment.

5. Analyze the data you have collected during the experiment.

6. Formulate a conclusion based on your research and the data you've gathered from your experiment.

7. Communicate your results to others who have an interest in the topic.

An example of scientific method is a very detailed step by step list of what must be considered and done when changing a lightbulb.

YourDictionary definition and usage example. Copyright © 2015 by LoveToKnow Corp

The website CARM has this to say.

What is the Scientific Method? by Matt Slick

The scientific method is used in science as a means of gaining understanding about the physical universe. There are differences of opinion on exactly what the scientific method is, but basically it consists of the following main parts.

1. Observation--a perception, viewing of a phenomena.

2. Hypothesis--a proposed explanation is developed to account what has been observed.

3. Experimentation--tests are developed to validate or invalidate the hypothesis.

4. Prediction--after tests and validation of the hypothesis, predictions are made based upon the evidence gathered in experimentation.

5. Theory--a theory is based upon a hypothesis, verified by testing, and is generally accepted as being an accurate explanation of phenomena.

So, with the scientific method, people attempt to understand something sufficiently to reproduce an event and/or accurately predict an event.

The exact order of the steps is fluid, but

generally the scientific method is the process used to understand phenomena through developing a hypothesis, experimentation, and learning, so that we are able to predict the phenomena again. This means the phenomena is understood.

Wikipedia explains further:

...that through observation and reproducible experimentation we can predict what will happen. The volume of positive outcomes may not prove it to be true but can add support to the theory. This proving of a hypothesis through experimentation builds trust that the hypotheses made were correct.

:This is an investigation of whether the real world behaves as predicted by the hypothesis. Scientists (and other people) test hypotheses by conducting experiments. The purpose of an experiment is to determine whether observations of the real world agree with or conflict with the predictions derived from an hypothesis. If they agree, confidence in the hypothesis increases; otherwise, it decreases. Agreement does not assure that the hypothesis is true; future experiments may reveal problems.

:A final point: a scientific hypothesis must be falsifiable, meaning that one can identify a possible outcome of an experiment that conflicts with predictions deduced from the hypothesis; otherwise, it cannot be meaningfully tested.

It seems to me, for the atheist to trust in the scientific method, when showing how our physical world works, it needs to be proven through experimentation. On the internet there are many good articles on how the physical universe got started. Some theories have a creator, others do not. To hold an informed opinion one would need to do at least some study on the subject.

Many brilliant minds have devoted their lives to the study of the beginning of everything. To quote just one;

'Astronomy leads us to a unique event, a universe which was created out of nothing, and delicately balanced to provide exactly the conditions required to support life. In the absence of an absurdly improbable accident, the observations of modern science seem to suggest an underlying, one might say, supernatural plan.'

- Nobel Prize-winning scientist Arno Penzias

When I look at both sides of this debate my tradesman mind keeps going back to the story of the Emperor's New Clothes. It took a small child to point out the fact that he was naked. Although atheists don't worship anything to be god, I believe these verses from Romans.1 apply.

Romans 1:20-22 KJV
20 For the invisible things of him from the

creation of the world are clearly seen, being understood by the things that are made, even his eternal power and Godhead; so that they are without excuse:

21 Because that, when they knew God, they glorified him not as God, neither were thankful; but became vain in their imaginations, and their foolish heart was darkened.

22 Professing themselves to be wise, they became fools,

I believe evolutionists must exercise as much faith to maintain their belief in a universe coming into existence from nothing, as I do believing that it was created by God. Trusting in the scientific reasoning used in the debate over the beginning of the universe gives no proven factual evidence as demanded for by the scientific method. Relegating the beginning of everything, to the time when the universe started taking on its physical form, is not the true beginning. Starting at a point when there was, if the theory is correct, gravity, with particles and antiparticles popping in and out of existence, is hardly a time when there was nothing. It may have been before the physical universe was brought into existence, but by saying something was there, says that something was there. Where did that something come from? You can't have a beginning to everything if something is already there. The scientific method deals with physical tangible objects and forces. Before you have them, you are in a realm outside of the scientific scope, that is where God dwells. Hope to the faithful evolutionist is left to unprovable possibilities and conjecture. For the evolutionist, as for myself, it is the faith in our beliefs that give us solace.

faith

fāTH/

noun

noun: faith

1. complete trust or confidence in someone or something.

"this restores one's faith in politicians"

synonyms: trust, belief, confidence,

conviction; More

optimism, hopefulness, hope

"he justified his boss's faith in him"

antonyms: mistrust

2. strong belief in God or in the doctrines of a religion, based on spiritual apprehension rather than proof.

synonyms: religion, church, sect, denomination, (religious) persuasion, (religious) belief, ideology, creed, teaching, doctrine

"she gave her life for her faith"

Where do Christians derive their faith? We may believe the scientific method is a useful tool in understanding how the world around us functions, but on what do we cling to as the source of our faith? As a biblist, I believe the word of God is given to us through the Bible. It is in the words and teachings of the Bible that I discover my source of faith, hope and trust. Hebrews 11:1-3

NCV puts it this way.

1 Faith means being sure of the things we hope for and knowing that something is real even if we do not see it.
2 Faith is the reason we remember great people who lived in the past.
3 It is by faith we understand that the whole world was made by God's command so what we see was made by something that cannot be seen.

Let me give you a few reasons why I feel so strongly that the teachings of the Bible are the best source for lifelong direction, and why I don't have that kind of faith in any other book or collection of teachings. Firstly I believe the Bible to be inspired by God. What makes me think that? One reason is the secular historical record showing the Bible's ability to reliably foretell the future. Not just in general terms, but very specifically, and well into the future.

The scripture written by Isaiah between (circa) 740-680 B.C., towards the end of the reign of

King Uzziah and throughout the reigns of King
Jotham, Ahaz and Hezekiah tell us of future
events.

Isaiah 44: 28 KJV
28 That saith of Cyrus, He is my shepherd,
and shall perform all my pleasure: even
saying to Jerusalem, Thou shalt be built;
and to the temple, Thy foundation shall be
laid.

No one knew who this Cyrus was at the time of
Isaiah's writing. Isaiah didn't apparently know
either. Isaiah was taking dictation from God. This
was God talking to his chosen nation of Israel
through Isaiah.

Isaiah 1:1-3 KJV
1 The vision of Isaiah the son of Amoz,
which he saw concerning Judah and
Jerusalem in the days of Uzziah, Jotham,
Ahaz, and Hezekiah, kings of Judah.
2 Hear, O heavens, and give ear, O earth:
for the LORD hath spoken, I have
nourished and brought up children, and
they have rebelled against me.

3 The ox knoweth his owner, and the ass his master's crib: but Israel doth not know, my people doth not consider.

Isaiah 8:1 KJV
8 Moreover the LORD said unto me, Take thee a great roll, and write in it with a man's pen concerning Mahershalalhashbaz.

These scriptures show that God was doing the dictation and Isaiah was doing the writing.

Secular history tells us that Cyrus the Great wasn't born till 600 BC a good eighty to one hundred and forty years after Isaiah wrote to the Jewish nation. He became a towering figure in history but he came from an obscure and tenuous start. Cyrus's own testimony tells us that he came from a royal family line. He was preceded as king of Persia by his father, grandfather and great-grandfather.

After Cyrus was born, Astyages the king had a dream, his wise men interpreted it as a sign that his grandson Cyrus would someday depose him. Fearing this he ordered his trusted servant Harpagus to kill the newborn Cyrus. Harpagus, who could not bear the thought of killing a baby, ordered Mardian Mitradates, a bandit herdsman from a mountainous area nearby, to leave Cyrus in the mountains to die. Having just lost their own child at birth the herdsman and his wife Spaca-o took Cyrus and raised him as their own, giving their own stillborn son as proof of Cyrus's death. Cyrus grows up as their son, he would have undoubtedly helped with the family business of herding animals. He grows in this environment into a strong noble boy. The deception is uncovered when Cyrus is ten, King Astyages allows him to come back to his rightful home and parents.

Ultimately Cyrus did overthrow his grandfather to become king in 559 BC. His kingdom was not an autonomous one as he still acknowledged the over-lordship of the Medians. He finally conquers the Median Empire in 549 BC. By 546 BC, he is crowned as the King of Persia galvanizing his complete rule. Culminating in the new Achaemenid Empire that will, under Cyrus, extend from Turkey, Asia Minor and Arabia in the west to the northwest regions of India in the east.

Cyrus cunningly takes over Babylon in 539 BC,

by diverting the Euphrates river, dropping the water level to the middle of a soldier's thigh. In October Cyrus and his army march into Babylon under the cover of darkness and take it with little to no resistance. It is not until this time that Cyrus would be in a position to fulfil the prophecy God had Isaiah record for him, almost two hundred years earlier.

In this Bible prophecy, as we have read, God specifically named Cyrus as the re-builder of Jerusalem. He calls Cyrus his shepherd, an even more appropriate description knowing how Cyrus was brought up as a child. For this prophecy to be fulfilled a great number of obstacles had to be overcome. From raising a ruler to have a shepherd's heart, to getting him into a position of power to do the job that God had called him to do. If God is not sovereign over the world and its systems, the possibility of Cyrus doing what God had specifically prophesied he would do, would have been unobtainable. For it to be predicted in such detail century's ahead of time proves to me the trustworthiness of the Bible.

At times people like to highlight the errors they

see in the Bible. It seems like their motives are to disprove the validity of the Bible and remove all faith in God. They don't try to explain the fulfilled prophecies like the one of Cyrus. If the detractors of the Bible and the God that it reveals, want to show how inaccurate and untrustworthy they both are, why not do something that God, through the Bible, has specifically said, would not happen?

It is one thing to predict some future event will happen. After all if you wait long enough someone, somewhere, at sometime in the future may do something close to what you said would happen. In his book Les Propheties, Nostradams makes some predictions of the future. Students of his book search through history for instances of one of his prophesies coming true, then proclaim how it was foretold ahead of time. A harder type of prophesy to make, is one where you say that something will never happen. Doing so restricts the people from the future, to the possibility of doing what you said could never happen. For instance, four thousand years ago it would have been a safe bet for God to have written in the Bible, "I have given the earth for man to live, and on it alone shall he walk, all the days of his life."

Bible believers would say, man will never walk on any other celestial body other than the earth. They would rightfully believe this to be a divine claim, made by God. The lunar landings and subsequent moon walks would ultimately prove God and his word wrong.

Limiting future events are wrought with failure because of the increasing knowledge and technology mankind is developing. Our modern gadgets are the fiction from previous generations. One would have to think long and hard before risking your reputation by predicting that something will not ever be done. But that is exactly what the God of the Bible has done. He has declared that something will never occur. More astounding, it is not something outlandishly impossible, like walking anywhere other than on the earth would have been before nineteen sixty nine. Rather it is something mundane, something mankind has a lot of experience doing.

God has declared that something seemingly very possible, will never happen. Why don't those who would like to disprove the Bible put their disbelief to a real life test and do what God has said will never be done? Like the prophecy involving Cyrus, Babylon again plays a central role. God has decreed that after being destroyed, Babylon shall never be re-inhabited. We read this in:

Isaiah 13:19-20 KJV
9 And Babylon, the glory of kingdoms, the beauty of the Chaldees' excellency, shall be as when God overthrew Sodom and Gomorrah.
20 It shall never be inhabited, neither shall it be dwelt in from generation to generation: neither shall the Arabian pitch tent there; neither shall the shepherds make their fold there.

It is repeated again by God in;

Jeremiah 50:39-40 KJV
39 Therefore the wild beasts of the desert with the wild beasts of the islands shall dwell there, and the owls shall dwell therein: and it shall be no more inhabited for ever; neither shall it be dwelt in from generation to generation.
40 As God overthrew Sodom and Gomorrah

and the neighbour cities thereof, saith the LORD; so shall no man abide there, neither shall any son of man dwell therein.

If your intent is to show how feeble and inaccurate God has been, in what some claim to be his revealed word the Bible, why not demonstrate God's impotence for all the world to see, by building a people filled, working, normal every day city on the site of ancient Babylon? It is in an area of the world where the Bible is not that popular right now. It's not as though the address has been lost, we all are capable of finding its precise location. Wouldn't doing what God has said will never be done, be a good demonstration of how Bible prophesies are illegitimate fakes? It wouldn't have to be anything fancy, perhaps a modest little city of ten or fifteen thousand.

Saddam Hussein started a rebuilding of Babylon back in 1983 although he had much loftier plans than a modest city. Ultimately Saddam's efforts came to nothing as the winds of change swept through his country. Saddam's grand palace was a ziggurat (stepped pyramid) in shape. No expense was spared in its lavish finishing, although the brick work of its structure was cracking with only ten years of service. After Saddam's fall from power, his rebuilding of ancient Babylon was plundered by the locals and denigrated by invading armies. His stately palace is now a hollow shell, much like the dream it was to be part of, the dream of a rebuilt Babylon. Why has this dream remained such an elusive one for the past millennia? The rebuilding of Babylon as a living city has been elusive to all that have tried for one main reason. God has declared that it will not be inhabited. It remains as empty today, as it will be in the future. This is another reason why I trust in what the Bible has to say to me. God is the only one that can reliably foretell the future with precise accuracy, as well as thwart the attempts of those who would do, what he has said, will never be accomplished.

As a biblist, my confidence in the Bible is strengthened by these prophecies. But as a Christian my hope, trust and faith come from no other source than Jesus. The Bible may give me a good source of understanding on how to live my life building my hope, trust and faith, but it is not essential to have or read the Bible to be a

Christian. The first gentile believers would not have had a Bible as we know it today. They had only the words of the apostles to build their hopes, trust and faith. Why would have those early gentiles believed the apostles?

I believe one reason, those early converts trusted the apostles stories about Jesus, came from a primal understanding of human nature. The apostles were the first ones to be taught by Jesus. They knew him personally, they were his constant companions for more than three years. They saw him be scourged and crucified. They were the ones that helped put him in the grave. They knew he had been killed and were afraid that they would be the next ones to die. They were afraid of their future and for their lives. Then three days later they stopped being afraid and hiding, and started to proclaim that the Jesus who had been crucified and died, had been resurrected and lived. They were now bold and out in the public hailing Jesus as the Messiah. No one convinced them of this, no one told them a story about Jesus. They were the first ones. If a false story was being told, it would have had to come from them. If the resurrection of Jesus was a lie, they would have been the ones that made it up.

This is where understanding our own human nature comes in. Con artists can convince us of most anything. People from all segments of society can be convinced, something that is a lie, is the truth. One thing remains constant though, the originator of the lie will know that it is a lie. Others that have been convinced of the lie may believe it to their death, they may willingly die for their belief in the lie. However the originator of the lie will know it is not true, and will not die for it. All of the apostles but John died a martyr's death, and John lived a martyr's life. The apostles would not have willingly been martyrs if they knew their faith in Jesus was a lie, that they themselves made up. Christian converts seeing the apostles die for their beliefs, were filled with the same faith, hope and trust in Jesus that the original apostles had. They could see the apostles faith, hope and trust was genuine if for no other reason than, you won't die, especially a gruesome martyrs death, for the sake of your own lie.

The faith in Jesus to save because he was the son of God. The hope of a new life at the resurrection.

These beliefs are what propelled Christianity from obscurity as a Jewish sect, to a world dominating religion. All that is done in the name of Christianity however, doesn't accurately reflect the teachings of Jesus. Some coming in the name of Jesus evoke his name to try and disguise who they are and what they do. Paul warned us this would happen.

Acts 20:29-31 KJV
29 For I know this, that after my departing shall grievous wolves enter in among you, not sparing the flock.
30 Also of your own selves shall men arise, speaking perverse things, to draw away disciples after them.
31 Therefore watch, and remember, that by the space of three years I ceased not to warn every one night and day with tears.

For those who look, the proofs given by God to guarantee Jesus was his son and our Savior, are still there in the scriptures for us to find. The Jewish leaders in the days of Jesus were watching for the messiah to come and restore Israel to worldly prominence. They had set out four miracles only the true messiah would be able to perform. They would check out the authenticity of the miracles and the miracle performer by observation and questioning. Although they had experiences of the dead being brought back to life, their tradition stated that a person could not be brought back to life after being dead for three full days. That kind of a resurrection would take the power of God. The scriptural source for the other three messianic miracles are:

Isaiah 35:5-6 KJV
5 Then the eyes of the blind shall be opened, and the ears of the deaf shall be unstopped.
6 Then shall the lame man leap as an hart, and the tongue of the dumb sing: for in the wilderness shall waters break out, and streams in the desert.

Over the centuries, while waiting for the messiah to come, the Jews came up with these miracles for the coming Messiah to do so they could recognize him and not be tricked by an imposter. These miracles were considered beyond the scope of human possibility and would require intervention from God to be performed. Performing these messianic miracles would prove the messiahship of the performer to the Jewish leaders. Anyone who performed these miracles would be welcomed as their messiah and leader. Jesus performed these four miracles openly for the Jewish leaders to see.

1) The Rabbis taught that only the Messiah could heal an Israelite leper.

2) The Rabbis taught that only the Messiah could cast out a mute demon.

3) The Rabbis taught that only the Messiah could heal a man born blind.

4) The Rabbis taught that only the Messiah could raise a man from the dead after four days.

It is important to keep in mind God did not claim these as the proofs for the messiah to do. These were miracles that the Rabbis came up with on their own, to satisfy themselves with the authenticity of their messiah. They wanted God to pass their tests to prove himself to them. Jesus did these test miracles for them, proving he was the true King of the Jews, as well as the true messiah for all of mankind.

The proof God gave to show Jesus was his son was less austere.

Isaiah 7: KJV
14 Therefore the Lord himself shall give you a sign; Behold, a virgin shall conceive, and bear a son, and shall call his name Emmanuel.

This sign from God of a virgin birth was definitely out of the ordinary, but was one that is hard to authenticate. It's not as though Mary had a doctor's note for proof of her virginity. For the people of the day, along with everyone since, we have no collaborating proof of Mary's virginity. We need to believe the stories or the written records that we have. God has declared in the Bible that Jesus was his son, however, God gave only one test proof Jesus was his son, that of a virgin birth.

Jesus gave a test proof to the Pharisees for a sign of his divinity and messiahship. Not only did he perform all of the messianic miracles required, he went on to expand the proofs of his messiahship.

He gave them the sign of Jonas. These people, who rejected Jesus and the messianic miracles he performed, were given a final test proof from Jesus himself. His final sign to them would be;

Matthew 12:38-42 KJV

38 Then certain of the scribes and of the Pharisees answered, saying, Master, we would see a sign from thee.

39 But he answered and said unto them, An evil and adulterous generation seeketh after a sign; and there shall no sign be given to it, but the sign of the prophet Jonas:

40 For as Jonas was three days and three nights in the whale's belly; so shall the Son of man be three days and three nights in the heart of the earth.

41 The men of Nineveh shall rise in judgment with this generation, and shall condemn it: because they repented at the preaching of Jonas; and, behold, a greater than Jonas is here.

42 The queen of the south shall rise up in the judgment with this generation, and

shall condemn it: for she came from the uttermost parts of the earth to hear the wisdom of Solomon; and, behold, a greater than Solomon is here.

Matthew 16:1-4 KJV

1 The Pharisees also with the Sadducees came, and tempting desired him that he would shew them a sign from heaven.

2 He answered and said unto them, When it is evening, ye say, It will be fair weather: for the sky is red.

3 And in the morning, It will be foul weather to day: for the sky is red and lowering. O ye hypocrites, ye can discern the face of the sky; but can ye not discern the signs of the times?

4 A wicked and adulterous generation seeketh after a sign; and there shall no sign be given unto it, but the sign of the prophet Jonas. And he left them, and departed.

Luke 11:28-32 KJV

28 But he said, Yea rather, blessed are they that hear the word of God, and keep it.

29 And when the people were gathered thick together, he began to say, This is an evil generation: they seek a sign; and there shall no sign be given it, but the sign of Jonas the prophet.

30 For as Jonas was a sign unto the Ninevites, so shall also the Son of man be to this generation.

31 The queen of the south shall rise up in the judgment with the men of this generation, and condemn them: for she came from the utmost parts of the earth to hear the wisdom of Solomon; and, behold, a greater than Solomon is here.

32 The men of Nineve shall rise up in the judgment with this generation, and shall condemn it: for they repented at the preaching of Jonas; and, behold, a greater than Jonas is here.

He gives them the sign of Jonas or Jonah. This sign would put Jesus in the grave for three days and three nights, just as Jonah was in the belly of the fish for three days and three nights. Then Jesus would be brought back to life.

Jonah 1:15-17 KJV

15 So they took up Jonah, and cast him forth into the sea: and the sea ceased from her raging.

16 Then the men feared the LORD exceedingly, and offered a sacrifice unto the LORD, and made vows.

17 Now the LORD had prepared a great fish to swallow up Jonah. And Jonah was in the belly of the fish three days and three nights.

Jesus told the religious leaders they could destroy the temple and that he would raise it back up in three days.

John 2:19-21 KJV

19 Jesus answered and said unto them, Destroy this temple, and in three days I will raise it up.

20 Then said the Jews, Forty and six years was this temple in building, and wilt thou rear it up in three days?

21 But he spake of the temple of his body.

This proof of Jesus went far beyond that of the

messianic miracles. Jesus was predicting that he would allow the Jews to beat and crucify him, be put into a grave, only to be raised back to life after three days and three nights. Then he would show himself to many witnesses for verification that he was alive. Now that was a test of messiahship the Jews had not thought of. Their messiah being willingly put to death, then coming back after being dead for a full three days, just to prove to them and mankind he was their legitimate King. Such a proof went far beyond any test the rabbis had thought of for the messiah to do. But that is exactly what Jesus did. Precisely as he said he would.

Jesus is our example to follow in this life. He showed us how we should live a life of love. He showed us how we should relate to our heavenly father. He showed us there is a resurrection from the dead. If we accept him and his atoning sacrifice for us, we can share with him eternal life in the kingdom of God. The disciples believed in and looked forward to this eternal life with him. They were there to hear Jesus explain when people would receive immortality and when he would raise up his believers to everlasting life. He

told the crowd four times when this
transformation would take place in John 6.

39 And this is the Father's will which hath
sent me, that of all which he hath given me
I should lose nothing, but should raise it up
again at the last day.
40 And this is the will of him that sent me,
that every one which seeth the Son, and
believeth on him, may have everlasting life:
and I will raise him up at the last day.

44 No man can come to me, except the
Father which hath sent me draw him: and
I will raise him up at the last day.

54 Whoso eateth my flesh, and drinketh my
blood, hath eternal life; and I will raise him
up at the last day.

Where Are They Now?

As a Christian I derive my faith in the trustworthiness of God. He is able to fulfil his promises to his adopted children, just as he was and is able to fulfil his prophecies of world events. My hope is rooted in Jesus and the sin cleansing sacrifice he made for all of mankind. My trust is in the example Jesus left, demonstrating a resurrection from the dead and a new type of body that is waiting for all who will believe in him. If you are not a Bible follower, understanding how the resurrections work can give hope and peace of mind to anyone who has lost a loved one. The resurrections of the Bible are not widely understood, but they provide a positive outcome for all who desire a loving relationship with their creator.

The resurrections, as I understand them to occur, are not universally believed in by all Christians, let alone other bodies of faith, or science.

Believers in a God of some type will give a bereaved parent more solace than that of the atheist, but the level of comfort will vary widely depending on the beliefs of the grieving parent and the religion they have faith in. There are many differing beliefs about the afterlife. Some faiths have faded from our view, they have been discarded and left behind as new concepts took their place. Old religions were replaced by more meaningful ones that connected with the followers psyche. A world changing movement began approximately two thousand years ago, it swept aside most all of the ancient religions around the Mediterranean sea. It spread rapidly through the population by personal testimonies and travelling evangelists. Two of the reasons for its success, was the promise of eternal life and a permanent home in a kingdom in which the believer was an heir to the ruling, God of love.

This new religion that burst onto the world stage was of course, Christianity. Today you will find within it a wide range of beliefs and traditions. The beliefs for what happens to a dead baby is no exception. Some will say that babies go directly to heaven when they die. As a rule this "Get out of jail (Hell)" card is reserved for people who have not reached an age of accountability for their decisions. They reason that God would not condemn a person to an eternity in hell if they were not, by way of maturity, responsible for themselves. They would get to bypass the pain and struggles of this life and go directly to heaven, spending eternity in the loving care of God. This seems like a pleasant thought to have for the unfortunate child.

Other Christians believe that the baby must go directly to hell. They explain that after the fall of man through Adam, all of mankind is doomed to the eternal torments of hell unless they personally accept the redemption that is only brought to us by Jesus. They say that without willingly believing on Jesus, sinful man can never dwell with God. They see man as sitting on the "Go directly to jail (Hell)" square.

Still others believe the baby's soul has to wait in a place until God decides the type of person the child would have grown into and then assign them to their appropriate fate. As you will find, if you do a bit of research, the opinions of believers under the Christian umbrella are vast. All will reference respected people, the Bible, or both to support their beliefs. I believe that if a person want's to understand what God has to tell us, they only have to look carefully into the Bible. I believe the Bible will not contradict itself and when it appears to be, we need to scrutinize the scriptures to find our misunderstanding. There are several points with the heaven, hell, or wait and see answers, that I feel conflict with the basic understandings of the Christian faith and Bible scriptures.

The need to personally accept Jesus.

If the baby goes to heaven when it dies, then the scriptures saying that the only way to obtain salvation is through willingly accepting Jesus would be untrue. The dead baby would have had no opportunity to develop a faith in Jesus or accept his salvation. If the baby goes directly to heaven when it dies, it makes a mockery of Jesus being the only way to salvation.

Acts 4:11-12 King James Version KJV
11 This is the stone which was set at nought of you builders, which is become the

head of the corner.

12 Neither is there salvation in any other: for there is none other name under heaven given among men, whereby we must be saved.

Ephesians 2:8 King James Version KJV
8 For by grace are ye saved through faith; and that not of yourselves: it is the gift of God:

John 3:15-18 KJV
15 That whosoever believeth in him should not perish, but have eternal life.
16 For God so loved the world, that he gave his only begotten Son, that whosoever believeth in him should not perish, but have everlasting life.
17 For God sent not his Son into the world to condemn the world; but that the world through him might be saved.
18 He that believeth on him is not condemned: but he that believeth not is condemned already, because he hath not believed in the name of the only begotten

Son of God.

Free moral agency.

Another problem with this common Christian belief is that the baby would have no opportunity to reject God and could be in heaven for all eternity against its will. You may think this to be a silly point, as no one would not want to be with God. We need only to look at the angels to see that this objection is false. The angels were with God in heaven and yet one third of them rejected him and followed Satan into a life of sin. The principle of free moral agency needs to be adhered to, otherwise God would be imposing himself onto the helpless babies. God is love, that is his nature and because of this he will let us choose to reject him if we want to.

1 John 4:8 KJV
8 He that loveth not knoweth not God; for God is love.

God is love and wants the best for us.

Relegating the baby to the tortures of hell has its problems as well. Where is the God of love that we have read about? He wants the best for us and it goes against his will that any should perish and not get to be with him.

2 Peter 3:9 KJV
9 The Lord is not slack concerning his promise, as some men count slackness; but is longsuffering to us-ward, not willing that any should perish, but that all should come to repentance.

God has planned out a path to salvation for all of humanity. He had eternity to do his planning so he could get the best return on the painful investment of his beloved sons death. It makes little sense God would have devised a plan where the returns of saved people would not be maximized. His investments will not return to him empty.

Isaiah 46:10 KJV
10 Declaring the end from the beginning, and from ancient times the things that are not yet done, saying, My counsel shall stand, and I will do all my pleasure:

Isaiah 55:11 KJV
11 So shall my word be that goeth forth out of my mouth: it shall not return unto me

void, but it shall accomplish that which I please, and it shall prosper in the thing whereto I sent it.

Believing in an in-between state where the baby would have to wait to find out their eternal fate, requires the believer to have a faith in tradition and dogma as strong or stronger than their faith in what the Bible has to say.

As a biblist, I find the answers for life's big questions contained in the Bible. The answers I find there are logical and not contradictory. I don't have to ignore one scripture to trust in another, nor do I take comfort in making a verse say, what I want it to say, by taking it out of its contextual meaning and intent. By freely letting the Bible speak, I find the answers to life's mysteries can be understood.

The Bible does not leave the fate of a dead baby in the dark, nor is it left to speculation with no clear outcome. A Google search will soon reveal many confident experts from all faiths telling you where most likely the dead baby is. They will use the wisdom of ancient scholars and texts to prove their opinion. Some will also use Bible scripture

My Baby Died. Where Is My Baby?

that demonstrates almost conclusively where the loved one probably is. This vagueness is not limited only to Christians but applies to other religions as well, especially if you ask about babies who have died, from faiths not of their own. I find the only opinion worth trusting in is the one God reveals through his word, the Bible.

To find the right answer though, we must go in the right direction. We must have our bearings set on the proper course at the start or we will be far from our desired destination in the end. If we start with wrong concepts we will not recognize the true answers when we see them. Knowing our human limitations is a must in order to find out where our beloved baby is.

Searching the Bible for, where are the dead babies of mankind, may give you an answer you do not want to hear. Having the background facts to properly understand and contextualize the information that is uncovered is essential. For instance, asking "Is my dead baby in heaven, or is it in hell?", demonstrates the need for a course adjustment. The question itself comes from a foundational misconception of mankind's true nature. The question presupposes that we have some sort of a spiritual, immortal life, innately within us. It assumes, as has most of humanity, that when we die physically we automatically go on to another state and continue to live, only in a different form, as a disembodied spirit. To be extremely physically handicapped as it were, but to be conscious and mentally aware of our surroundings whatever they may be. Becoming a disembodied spirit seems to be the predominant thought throughout mankind's history.

Where did this concept of immortal spirit life come from and why is it so universally accepted and prevalent throughout all the cultures and varied religions of the world? If it was a concept taught only in the Bible, then it would not be found in other religions that don't recognize the Bible as the truth of God. They would have their own ideas about the nature of man. For all of humanity to share the same basic idea of an "immortal soul", shows that the idea began at the start of mankind and was then kept as a truth by the ever expanding and diversifying population, cultures and religions.

As I have pointed out before, the Bible will give us answers to the big questions in life if we are willing to let it speak to us. The Bible records what happened at the very start of mankind and how we were led away from God. It gives us insight into our nature few recognize. The Bible tells us in Genesis 2:7 that God created man as a physical being made out of the dust of the earth.

7 And the Lord God formed man of the dust of the ground, and breathed into his nostrils the breath of life; and man became a living soul.

The term soul comes from the Hebrew word nephesh, used to describe all physical life, Strong's concordance shows this to be a fact.

nephesh

neh'-fesh

properly a breathing creature, that is, animal or (abstractly) vitality; used very widely in a literal, accommodated or figurative sense (bodily or mental)

KJV Usage: any, appetite, beast, body,

breath, creature, X dead (-ly), desire, X [dis-] contented, X fish, ghost, + greedy, he, heart (-y), (hath, X jeopardy of) life (X in jeopardy), lust, man, me, mind, mortality. one, own, person, pleasure, (her-, him-, my-, thy-) self, them (your) -selves, + slay, soul, + tablet, they, thing, (X she) will, X would have it.

We see the word soul describes our emotions and body, it was never used to mean immortal, or to say there is a spiritual part of us that will live separate from our physical bodies. In fact, it's used to say the exact opposite, as I showed in bold print, the KJV translators used the word soul to define man as a, mortal, being.

Brown-Driver-Briggs' Hebrew Definitions

נֶפֶשׁ

1. soul, self, life, creature, person, appetite, mind, living being, desire, emotion, passion

a. that which breathes, the breathing substance or being, soul, the inner being of man

b. living being

c. living being (with life in the blood)

d. the man himself, self, person or individual

e. seat of the appetites

f. seat of emotions and passions

g. activity of mind

1. dubious

h. activity of the will

1. dubious

i. activity of the character

Later on in Genesis 3:22-24 God keeps man out of the garden of Eden so he cannot eat of the tree of life and gain immortality. Had God created man with an immortal soul, it would have done no good to keep him from the tree of life, as immortality would already be in his possession.

22 And the LORD God said, Behold, the man is become as one of us, to know good and evil: and now, lest he put forth his hand, and take also of the tree of life, and eat, and live for ever:
23 Therefore the LORD God sent him forth from the garden of Eden, to till the ground from whence he was taken.
24 So he drove out the man; and he placed at the east of the garden of Eden Cherubims, and a flaming sword which turned every way, to keep the way of the tree of life.

When you look for them, you will find many other verses in the Bible that show mankind is mortal and does not have an eternal soul, or spirit, as most religions believe. To find how mankind started to believe they had an eternal spirit, a consciousness that does not die, we again can turn to the Bible for the answer. Genesis 3:1-5 tells us clearly about the occurrence. The first lie recorded in the Bible is here. It comes from the father of lies and it has been believed by mankind ever since. It is the lie that has sent us in the wrong direction when we are looking for the answers to life and death. To arrive at our desired destination we need to start off in the right direction. Verse 4 shows the lie cleverly wrapped in the truth of how to become wise. Because the lie was believed at the beginning of humanity, it has infected all civilizations and faiths ever since and is still thriving today.

Genesis 3:1-5 KJV
3 Now the serpent was more subtil than any beast of the field which the LORD God had made. And he said unto the woman, Yea, hath God said, Ye shall not eat of every tree of the garden?
2 And the woman said unto the serpent, We may eat of the fruit of the trees of the garden:
3 But of the fruit of the tree which is in the midst of the garden, God hath said, Ye shall not eat of it, neither shall ye touch it, lest ye die.
4 And the serpent said unto the woman, Ye shall not surely die:

5 For God doth know that in the day ye eat thereof, then your eyes shall be opened, and ye shall be as gods, knowing good and evil.

When we think about what the words die and live mean, they are similar to light and dark, in that they are opposites. You can't have, or be one and the other at the same time. You can't quantify or measure dark, or dead. We can measure life and light, the amount, as well as its intensity. Dark is the absence of light. Absolute darkness is the total absence of light. We don't say there is only two candle powers of darkness, we say that about how much light a candle produces.

In the same way, we don't measure dead. We take the measurable signs of life such as breathing, pulse, electrical brain activity and our emotions. All are encompassed in life and are measurements of it. Being dead takes all of these attributes away. The person is left with none of the things that would make them alive. To have just a faint pulse, or an electrical current in your heart or brain would make you barely alive, but there still may be a chance for survival. If the person was brought back from the brink of death, they will live. If they are not and they lose their life signs, they will be dead.

The Bible describes death in Ecclesiastes as not being aware of anything, decaying back to our original components the same as all physical earthly life does.

Ecclesiastes 3:19-20 KJV
19 For that which befalleth the sons of men befalleth beasts; even one thing befalleth them: as the one dieth, so dieth the other; yea, they have all one breath; so that a man hath no preeminence above a beast: for all is vanity.
20 All go unto one place; all are of the dust, and all turn to dust again.

Ecclesiastes 9:5-6 KJV
5 For the living know that they shall die: but the dead know not any thing, neither have they any more a reward; for the memory of them is forgotten.
6 Also their love, and their hatred, and their envy, is now perished; neither have

they any more a portion for ever in any thing that is done under the sun.

The baby that has died is just that, dead. It's not in heaven, nor is it, as some will contend, in hell. Nor is it, in an in between state, waiting to go to its final destination. It would need to have immortality to be in any of these places. The child is asleep in its grave now, just as we are told David and Solomon are.

1 Kings 11:43 KJV
43 And Solomon slept with his fathers, and was buried in the city of David his father: and Rehoboam his son reigned in his stead.

1 Kings 2:10 KJV
10 So David slept with his fathers, and was buried in the city of David.

The baby is asleep, like many of the eyewitnesses to the resurrection of Jesus are asleep, as referred to by Paul. The believers from generations past have fallen asleep, as we have already read they are waiting to be awakened by Jesus when he returns at the last day.

1 Corinthians 15:4-6 KJV

4 And that he was buried, and that he rose again the third day according to the scriptures:

5 And that he was seen of Cephas, then of the twelve:

6 After that, he was seen of above five hundred brethren at once; of whom the greater part remain unto this present, but some are fallen asleep.

The grave is not the final home for the baby as there is a bright future awaiting it. God has promised to resurrect the dead. In their upcoming resurrected life, those who died not having the chance to accept Jesus, will be given that opportunity. Abraham knew God was able to raise the dead and was not afraid to sacrifice his son as he had been instructed.

Hebrews 11:19 KJV

19 Accounting that God was able to raise him up, even from the dead; from whence also he received him in a figure.

God has promised that he will resurrect us. He will bring mankind back to life in a resurrection from the dead. One of the places a resurrection is mentioned in the Bible is in:

Isaiah 26:19 KJV
19 Thy dead men shall live, together with my dead body shall they arise. Awake and sing, ye that dwell in dust: for thy dew is as the dew of herbs, and the earth shall cast out the dead.

All people will be resurrected, some to glory, some to shame, some to have their first chance to know Jesus. Being mortal by nature we require God to bring us back to life, God assured us he knows us intimately and will not forget us.

Isaiah 49:15 English Standard Version
15 "Can a woman forget her nursing child, that she should have no compassion on the son of her womb? Even these may forget, yet I will not forget you.

Isaiah 44:24 TLB
24 The Lord, your Redeemer who made you, says: All things were made by me; I

alone stretched out the heavens. By myself I made the earth and everything in it.

We can be confident in God's ability to resurrect us, just as he took care to create David inside his mother, as described in:

Psalm 139:13-18 NIV
13 For you created my inmost being; you knit me together in my mother's womb.
14 I praise you because I am fearfully and wonderfully made; your works are wonderful, I know that full well.
15 My frame was not hidden from you when I was made in the secret place, when I was woven together in the depths of the earth.
16 Your eyes saw my unformed body; all the days ordained for me were written in your book before one of them came to be.
17 How precious to me are your thoughts, God! How vast is the sum of them!
18 Were I to count them, they would outnumber the grains of sand—when I awake, I am still with you.

All people will have an opportunity to follow Jesus. Only those who have faith in Jesus will receive eternal life, those who reject Jesus will not, they will die. The opposite of life is death, this death will be permanent as the only source to life through Jesus has been rejected by them. If they reject life, it will be their free will choice. God will honour their decision to die.

John 3:16 KJV
16 For God so loved the world, that he gave his only begotten Son, that whosoever believeth in him should not perish, but have everlasting life.

Romans 6:23KJV
23 For the wages of sin is death; but the gift of God is eternal life through Jesus Christ our Lord.

Overview of Mankind's Resurrections

All of the believers of Jesus who die in this life, will sleep in their graves, like those in Corinth did. Today's followers of Jesus have always wanted to know when they will be transformed into their Spiritual form. At his return, all that are his will be raised to join him in the air as he comes back to the world as its sovereign king. Jesus repeatedly and plainly told his followers as we read in John 6, transformation will take place at the last day. When those believers are resurrected to their new life at the return of Jesus, they will rule with him as kings and priests.

We are given more information about the last day in 1 Thessalonians. Here, the birth of those called by God and have overcome the world and the temptations of Satan, is being described to us. They will meet Jesus in the air at his return, just as he promised. Those that are asleep will rise first, followed by the saints that are alive at his coming.

1 Thessalonians 4:16-17 New Century
Version
16 The Lord himself will come down from
heaven with a loud command, with the
voice of the archangel, and with the
trumpet call of God. And those who have
died believing in Christ will rise first.
17 After that, we who are still alive will be
gathered up with them in the clouds to
meet the Lord in the air. And we will be
with the Lord forever.

When those believers are resurrected to their new
life at the return of Jesus, they rule with him as
kings and priests. Having built Godly spiritual
muscle by resisting sin in their physical lives, they
reign with Jesus as the earth is refreshed after its
denigration by humanity. At the end time, when
Jesus returns, the world's capacity to support life
will have come to an end. We are told this in:

Matthew 24:22 New King James Version.
22 And unless those days were shortened,
no flesh would be saved; but for the elect's

sake those days will be shortened.

Restoration of the planet will take a thousand years. As we read in Revelation 20:5 it is not until the thousand years are over that the rest of the dead, including the babies who have died before they knew of, or could accept Jesus, experience their own resurrection. All the dead babies of humanity, along with those who have never had an opportunity to willingly choose Jesus in this life, will remain in their graves until this time of restoration is completed. They will be resurrected to a physical life like we have today. They will have a hundred year long life to live on the newly rejuvenated planet. God is not a pushy, hard sell, salesman. This hundred year long life will give them their opportunity to learn of Jesus, being taught and led by those believers resurrected at the return of Jesus. The majority of humanity will now have to decide for themselves if they want to follow Jesus or not.

Revelation 20:5 KJV
5 But the rest of the dead lived not again until the thousand years were finished. This is the first resurrection.

Isaiah 65:20 KJV

20 There shall be no more thence an infant of days, nor an old man that hath not filled his days: for the child shall die an hundred years old; but the sinner being an hundred years old shall be accursed.

The babies will get to mature and develop into the person they choose to become. Raised by the adults and families that are resurrected at the same time, the babies will live out their newly resurrected lives here on the freshly transformed earth. The life choices they make will be theirs alone as the Satanic influence to sin will not be present, but they will be guided by the Christian kings and priests who were resurrected at the return of Jesus. Satan is to be chained up in a pit until the thousand years of restoration are complete and the hundred year life span of the newly resurrected comes to a close.

God will not force anyone into accepting him and no one will get to live with him without going through Jesus. Should the people in this resurrection decide not to choose Jesus before they die, their death will be their end. As the Bible states several times the only way to gain eternal life is to believe in Jesus, by not accepting Jesus they will have willingly rejected Jesus and eternal life. There will not be another opportunity for them to be resurrected as they will have had their one chance to choose Jesus unencumbered. The way to eternal life is through Jesus alone. Humanity's fate is decided by them and their decision to reject Jesus will be respected by God for the rest of eternity and they will remain dead.

John 14:6 KJV
6 Jesus saith unto him, I am the way, the truth, and the life: no man cometh unto the Father, but by me.

There is one more resurrection to take place just before God comes to dwell with his new family. This final resurrection is for those who were called and had their opportunity to come to Jesus during this present life, or had their faith accounted unto them as righteousness, but for some reason they ended up rejecting Jesus.

John 12:42-43 The Message
42-43 On the other hand, a considerable

number from the ranks of the leaders did believe. But because of the Pharisees, they didn't come out in the open with it. They were afraid of getting kicked out of the meeting place. When push came to shove they cared more for human approval than for God's glory.

Matthew 10:32-33 Good News Translation
32 "Those who declare publicly that they belong to me, I will do the same for them before my Father in heaven.
33 But those who reject me publicly, I will reject before my Father in heaven.

The people who are brought back in this last resurrection have turned their backs on God and Jesus. These are the ones who, like Satan, choose to sin willfully. All will have to give an account for themselves and be judged. They will be resurrected as mortal beings and when they are thrown into the lake of fire, they will be destroyed by it and die.

Revelation 20:11-15 King James Version
11 And I saw a great white throne, and him

that sat on it, from whose face the earth and the heaven fled away; and there was found no place for them.

12 And I saw the dead, small and great, stand before God; and the books were opened: and another book was opened, which is the book of life: and the dead were judged out of those things which were written in the books, according to their works.

13 And the sea gave up the dead which were in it; and death and hell delivered up the dead which were in them: and they were judged every man according to their works.

14 And death and hell were cast into the lake of fire. This is the second death.

15 And whosoever was not found written in the book of life was cast into the lake of fire.

They may know Jesus and be fully expecting to enter into God's Kingdom only to find they have been rejected.

Matthew 7:21-23 Easy-to-Read Version
21 "Not everyone who calls me Lord will
enter God's Kingdom. The only people who
will enter are those who do what my Father
in heaven wants.
22 On that last Day many will call me
Lord. They will say, 'Lord, Lord, by the
power of your name we spoke for God. And
by your name we forced out demons and
did many miracles.'
23 Then I will tell those people clearly, 'Get
away from me, you people who do wrong. I
never knew you.'

Matthew 13:24-30 Living Bible
24 Here is another illustration Jesus used:
"The Kingdom of Heaven is like a farmer
sowing good seed in his field;
25 but one night as he slept, his enemy
came and sowed thistles among the wheat.
26 When the crop began to grow, the
thistles grew too.
27 "The farmer's men came and told him,
'Sir, the field where you planted that choice
seed is full of thistles!'

28 "'An enemy has done it,' he exclaimed.

"'Shall we pull out the thistles?' they asked.
29 "'No,' he replied. 'You'll hurt the wheat if you do.
30 Let both grow together until the harvest, and I will tell the reapers to sort out the thistles and burn them, and put the wheat in the barn.'"

Being mortal when they are burned they will die in the flames. They will become ashes under the feet of the saints. Their punishment will last for the rest of eternity as they will never be resurrected to life again. They will not be in eternal punishing, but their punishment will last for eternity.

Malachi 4:1-3 Easy-to-Read Version
1 "That time of judgment is coming. It will be like a hot furnace. All the proud people will be punished. All the evil people will burn like straw. At that time they will be like a bush burning in the fire, and there will not be a branch or root left." This is what the LORD All-Powerful said.

2 "But, for my followers, goodness will shine on you like the rising sun. And it will bring healing power like the sun's rays. You will be free and happy, like calves freed from their stalls.
3 Then you will walk on the evil people— they will be like ashes under your feet. I will make this happen at the time of judgment." This is what the LORD All-Powerful said.

Satan however, is not mortal. He is a spirit being, who has immortality. When he is cast into the lake of fire, he will be tormented there for the rest of eternity. The next time Satan reminds you of your past, remind him of his future.

Revelation 20:10 King James Version
10 And the devil that deceived them was cast into the lake of fire and brimstone, where the beast and the false prophet are, and shall be tormented day and night for ever and ever.

The thought of our dead babies safe with Jesus can be a comforting one until you start to work through all the ramifications that it brings.

Do they get to exercise their free will of choice or are they destined to possibly be with God against their will? The angels were safe with God and yet one third of them ultimately rejected him.

Where do the babies get their immortality from to be with God, if it comes exclusively through accepting Jesus?

Some will tell us the babies are in heaven because they had not yet reached an age of accountability. If that is true how can they be deemed sufficiently accountable to accept Jesus which is the only way to obtain eternal life?

The unpleasant thought of them being tormented in the fires of hell is just as tenuous. How did they gain the eternal life that would be required for them to be there for all eternity? To have eternal life we must believe in Jesus, when we believe in Jesus we stay out of hell.

Why would God conceive of and put into motion a plan where he would lose a large percentage of humanity, his future children, after all he is a God of love?

The uncertain future of babies being in a place to await their ultimate fate is equally unsettling for the grieving parent as some or all of the above questions may still persist in the parents minds.

Some may scoff at this understanding of the scriptures and resurrection, thinking it gives people a second chance at salvation. This is not a second chance to come to Jesus, but rather the first opportunity for most to learn of Jesus and the life giving salvation found only in him. I find the resurrections as described to be the only scripturally based way for all people to receive salvation, who for whatever reason did not have the opportunity to accept Jesus during this present life, especially helpless babies. When we look into the Bible, it shows us how all people will have a chance to choose God's way of life through Jesus and obtain eternal life.

God gives us freedom of thought in the peripheral areas of the Christian faith. That is why there are so many different Christian denominations, all worshipping God, all finding access to him through the saving grace of his Christ. If you find solace in a particular belief and you are satisfied that it is accurate, then that is your truth. If your heart felt belief turns out to be inaccurate, when you reach your final destination, it is not likely to make much difference in God's plan for your life. Knowing the options that are out there for us to believe in, can strengthen our convictions in what we find to be true, or can show us a better way. Like the Christians in Berea we should search the scriptures to be sure our faith has a strong foundation.

Acts 17:11 Easy-to-Read Version

The people in Berea were more open-minded than those in Thessalonica. They were so glad to hear the message Paul told them. They studied the Scriptures every day to make sure that what they heard was really true.

"Where is my dead baby?" is not a question that a grieving parent will want to leave unanswered. I think we all want to know our beliefs are set on sure foundations. As a biblist, I try to let the word of God be my sure foundation in all aspects of life. Within the Bible God shows us his plan for humanities salvation. I wrote this short book, for a glimpse into that salvation plan for all who have suffered the loss of loved ones. Our creator has salvation ready for them, if they decide to accept it. If you do not have a sure foundation for your beliefs or if you ponder the fate of dead babies, I hope you take the time to study the Bible and find the comfort God has placed there, when answering the big mysteries of life.

About The Author

Clayton and his wife live in the Okanagan Valley of southern British Colombia, Canada. They have two adult children and enjoy getting out to explore the outdoors, camping and quading. Clayton started his working career as an owner-operator in the trucking industry. After an industrial accident he retrained as a heavy duty mechanic and driving instructor. He enjoys working with his hands. Being a tradesman provides a good living for his family, but his passion is to study the Bible as the Bereans did, proving what is true from the scriptures.

Clayton is a published freelance author within the Christian genre. He writes articles and bible studies for the www.Biblists.com web site, and has audio books and articles appearing on various podcast websites.

Join Clayton and team in the Berean tradition, as they find biblical truth. Understanding scripture by reviewing original texts of ancient believers, scrutinizing modern theology.

Connect with Clayton B Carlson

I really appreciate you reading my book!

Find me on Facebook:
https://www.facebook.com/biblists/
Visit my website: www.Biblists.com

Books by Clayton B Carlson

Biblist Apologetics
My Baby Died. Where is My Baby?
Searching For Immortality
The Eden Conspiracy
Thy Kingdom Come, The Next Big Thing.

www.ingramcontent.com/pod-product-compliance
Lightning Source LLC
Chambersburg PA
CBHW060659030426
42337CB00017B/2689